CORNERSTONES OF FREEDOM™

The FRENCH AND INDIAN WAR

BY ANDREW SANTELLA

CHILDREN'S PRESS®
An Imprint of Scholastic Inc.
New York Toronto London Auckland Sydney
Mexico City New Delhi Hong Kong
Danbury, Connecticut

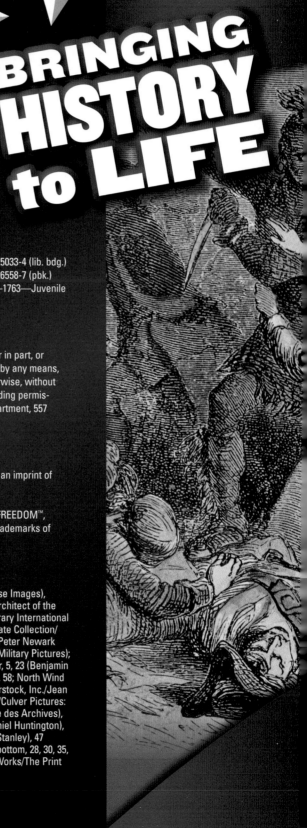

Content Consultant
Evan Haefeli, PhD
Assistant Professor of History
Columbia University
New York, New York

Library of Congress Cataloging-in-Publication Data
Santella, Andrew.
    The French and Indian War/by Andrew Santella.
        p. cm.—(Cornerstones of freedom)
    Includes bibliographical references and index.
    ISBN-13: 978-0-531-25033-4 (lib. bdg.)   ISBN-10: 0-531-25033-4 (lib. bdg.)
    ISBN-13: 978-0-531-26558-1 (pbk.)   ISBN-10: 0-531-26558-7 (pbk.)
    1. United States—History—French and Indian War, 1755–1763—Juvenile
literature. I. Title. II. Series.
    E199.S23 2012
    973.26—dc22   2011011972

1 2 3 4 5 6 7 8 9 10 R 21 20 19 18 17 16 15 14 13 12

Photographs © 2012: Alamy Images: 4 bottom, 34 (Ivy Close Images),
16 (North Wind Picture Archives); Andrew Santella: 64; Architect of the
Capitol, Washington, DC/Allyn Cox: 22; Bridgeman Art Library International
Ltd., London/New York: 25, 57 (Charles Willson Peale/Private Collection/
Peter Newark American Pictures), 20 (Private Collection/Peter Newark
American Pictures), 27 (Private Collection/Peter Newark Military Pictures);
Library of Congress: 38 (Pierre Charles Canot), back cover, 5, 23 (Benjamin
Franklin), 12 (Jan Van Vianen), 48 (William Woollett), 8, 44, 58; North Wind
Picture Archives: 14, 32; Ohio Historical Society: 13; Superstock, Inc./Jean
Leon Gerome Ferris: cover; The Art Archive/Picture Desk/Culver Pictures:
29; The Granger Collection, New York: 33 (Henri Beau/Rue des Archives),
11 (Felix O.C. Darley), 37 (William Hoare), 4 center, 15 (Daniel Huntington),
7 (Charles W. Jefferys), 45 (J.S.C. Schaak), 51 (John Mix Stanley), 47
(Augustus Tholey), 2, 3, 4 top, 10, 17, 18, 19, 24, 26 top, 26 bottom, 28, 30, 35,
36, 39, 41, 42, 46, 50, 54, 56 bottom, 56 top, 59; The Image Works/The Print
Collector/Heritage: 40.

Did you know that studying history can be fun?

BRING HISTORY TO LIFE by becoming a history investigator. Examine the evidence (primary and secondary source materials); cross-examine the people and witnesses. Take a look at what was happening at the time—but be careful! What happened years ago might suddenly become incredibly interesting and change the way you think!

Contents

JOIN, or DIE.

Conflict in North America

To the powerful nations of Europe, North America was a prize to be won. They were willing to fight to win it. In the 16th century, settlers from England, France, Spain, and other countries were drawn to North America by its great natural wealth. European rulers began establishing **colonies** in North America. They hoped to make their countries richer.

By the 1700s, France and Great Britain had emerged as the two strongest European powers in North America. France had established colonies in Canada and Louisiana. It sent traders and **missionaries** deep into the continent. Great Britain's North American colonies were confined to a narrow strip east of the Appalachian Mountains. There they developed an agricultural economy driven by slave labor.

Hundreds of different Native American peoples had lived in North America long before the arrival of Europeans. They had their own traditions and ways of life.

Quebec was one of the earliest French settlements in Canada.

Both France and England tried to win the natives' support to gain an advantage in their fight for North America. Algonquian-speaking natives of the northern woodlands became allies of the French. The British allied with the Iroquois Confederacy. The Iroquois were famed for their military might.

British settlements began moving farther west into the continent as more colonists arrived. The French built forts along the western frontier of the British colonies. They hoped to contain the spread. Major conflict soon became inevitable.

WAR LASTED NINE YEARS.

CHAPTER 1

THE BEAUTIFUL RIVER

Jacques Cartier was the first French explorer in North America.

FRENCH EXPLORERS FIRST visited North America in 1534. Jacques Cartier sailed up the St. Lawrence River to the site of modern-day Montreal. Traders and missionaries soon followed. They pushed deep into the continent. Native Americans taught them to use lightweight birch-bark canoes. This allowed them to travel along rivers as if they were watery highways. The French traded and formed **alliances** with Native Americans as they pushed farther into the continent. French missionaries sought to convert the native people to the Catholic faith. The French built chains of forts along major rivers to protect their trade routes. By the 1700s, New France extended from Canada across the Great Lakes and down the Mississippi River to the Gulf of Mexico.

Jamestown was the first permanent British settlement in North America.

Great Britain's colonies were largely restricted to the land between the Atlantic Ocean and the Appalachian Mountains. The first British colony in North America was founded in 1607 at Jamestown, Virginia. Colonists continued to arrive in large numbers for the next 150 years or so. The population of Great Britain's North American colonies was 20 times as large as that of New France by the mid-1700s. British colonists looked west for new places to settle as their numbers grew.

A FIRSTHAND LOOK AT
A PRISONER'S TALE

On February 29, 1704, the Reverend John Williams of Deerfield, Massachusetts, was taken captive by French soldiers during an attack on his hometown. He was marched north to Canada with other captives. He was able to return home two years later. He published a book about his experience called *The Redeemed Captive Returning to Zion*. See page 60 for a link to read excerpts from the book online.

British and French expansion led both groups of settlers to the same place. In what is now western Pennsylvania, a river begins a 981-mile (1,579 kilometer) run westward. The French called it *la Belle Riviere*, "the beautiful river." The Iroquois called it *Ohio*, "the great river."

The British and French both hoped to gain control of the Ohio River.

Céloron de Blainville claimed the Ohio River valley for France.

The Value of the Valley

The French saw the Ohio River as an important water route westward into the interior of North America. French explorer René-Robert Cavelier, Sieur de La Salle first claimed the river for France in 1669.

The French wanted to keep the river out of the hands of the British. In 1749, French officials sent an expedition led by Pierre-Joseph Céloron de Blainville into the Ohio River valley. Céloron de Blainville buried lead tablets along the river's banks stating that the area was French territory.

These lead tablets did little to keep British colonists out of the area. British colonial leaders believed that the Ohio country belonged to them. There were many native people living in the Ohio River valley. But King George II of England had given a group called the Ohio Company permission to build a settlement there.

This was welcome news to British colonists. Land in the east had become hard to find as their numbers grew. The British tobacco plantations used up huge amounts of land and needed constant expansion. More and more slaves were brought into the colonies to work on ever-larger plantations. This added to the need for more space. The Ohio River valley offered the British colonies

The French property tablets did not convince the British to leave the Ohio River valley.

room to grow. The Ohio Company sent a surveyor named Christopher Gist to explore the valley. His job was to find the best spots for forts and settlements.

A third group was also ready to fight for the valley. The Iroquois Confederacy had been launching raids against neighboring tribes around the Great Lakes for more than a century. They attacked Algonquian-speaking tribes so fiercely that much of the continent came to fear Iroquois war parties. The Iroquois's power extended into the Ohio River valley. They would have a say in anything that happened there.

Christopher Gist explored the land along the Ohio River.

Gist guided George Washington on his journey to Fort LeBoeuf.

Washington's Message

In 1753, France began building a string of forts between Lake Erie and the Ohio River. The forts were intended to give France control over the region. But British colonists were not about to give up their own plans for the valley. The lieutenant governor of the Virginia Colony, Robert Dinwiddie, sent a messenger to the French at Fort LeBoeuf, near Lake Erie. The messenger's name was George Washington. Washington carried a letter explaining that the French were trespassing on British territory. It demanded that they leave the area as quickly as possible.

Washington was a 21-year-old major in the Virginia **militia** and loyal to Great Britain. It took him two and a half months to travel from Virginia to Fort LeBoeuf and

The French officers at Fort LeBoeuf refused the British demands that they leave the territory.

back. He nearly drowned trying to cross an icy river on his return trip. He had bad news for Dinwiddie when he returned to Virginia. The French had refused to leave the Ohio River valley.

Washington also reported another bit of important news. He had come upon an ideal location for a fort to protect British traders and settlers during his trip. It would stand at a place called the Forks of the Ohio. There the Allegheny and Monongahela Rivers come together to form the Ohio River.

Dinwiddie liked the idea of building a fort at the Forks of the Ohio. He promoted Washington to lieutenant colonel. He also told him to organize a force of about 120 soldiers to cut a road through the thick forest between Virginia and the Forks. The road would be wide enough for wagons to carry supplies and cannons to the new British fort. A group of woodsmen from Virginia made their way to the Forks in April 1754 and began building a **stockade** there.

Shots Fired

The French were on their way to build their own fort at the Forks of the Ohio at the

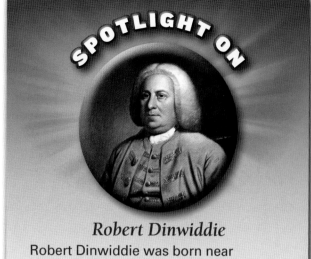

SPOTLIGHT ON

Robert Dinwiddie

Robert Dinwiddie was born near Glasgow, Scotland, in 1693. Dinwiddie worked as a merchant and a British tax collector before coming to Virginia. He was named lieutenant governor of the Virginia Colony in 1751.

Colonial governors did not take an active role in governing their territories at the time. But the lieutenant governors did. Dinwiddie's new position put him in charge of the colony. He returned to England midway through the French and Indian War and retired from government service.

same time. A French force of 500 well-armed soldiers chased off the Virginians and took control of the Forks. They constructed Fort Duquesne and named it after the governor-general of New France.

Washington and his troops followed orders and pushed on toward the Forks. Washington's Indian allies urged him to attack the French. Tanaghrisson was a leader of the Seneca nation. He told Washington that a small group of

Washington ordered his men to launch a surprise attack on the French soldiers.

French soldiers was camped nearby and could easily be surprised.

Washington's troops found 35 French soldiers camped in a hollow on the morning of May 28. They were preparing their breakfasts. Washington and his troops surrounded the French and opened fire. The ambush lasted just 15 minutes. Washington and his men killed 12 French soldiers, including their commander, Joseph Coulon de Villiers, Sieur de Jumonville. A few French soldiers managed to escape and hurry back to safety at Fort Duquesne. Washington knew that more French troops would come looking for revenge when they found out what had happened that morning.

Washington retreated to a place called the Great Meadows. He ordered his troops to build a crude, circular stockade and named it Fort Necessity. The fort offered little protection to Washington's force. More than 500 French soldiers and 100 of their native allies arrived outside Fort Necessity on July 3. They took positions on high ground and began firing down on Fort Necessity. Washington lost 31 men and was ready to surrender by nightfall.

The victorious French allowed Washington and his surviving troops to return to Virginia. But first, the French made Washington sign a paper admitting to the assassination of Jumonville during the previous month's ambush. The first shots had been fired in a war that would soon spread around the world.

YESTERDAY'S HEADLINES

Washington's attack on Jumonville and his men was a major scandal in France. The French became outraged at Washington's actions as news of the attack spread throughout the country. France and Great Britain had not been at war when Washington launched his ambush. This made the attack illegal. The incident was used as propaganda to drum up support in France for a full-scale war against the British. Washington was portrayed as a villain in French news reports.

CHAPTER 2

A FIGHT IN THE WILDERNESS

Iroquois representatives met with British leaders in New York in 1754.

WAR WAS BREWING IN THE
Ohio River valley. The leaders of the British colonies
wanted to protect themselves from French attacks.
In 1754, seven of the 13 colonies agreed to send
representatives to Albany, New York, to discuss
defense plans. They also invited representatives from
the Iroquois nations. The British wanted the help of
Iroquois warriors if full-scale war broke out. They
also wanted to purchase land from the Iroquois.

The colonists lavished the Iroquois with gifts
such as food, clothing, and jewelry. The Iroquois
gladly accepted the gifts. But they were unsure
about taking Great Britain's side in a war against
the French. They wanted to be sure that the British
could defeat the French. The Iroquois promised
only that they would remain **neutral**.

The meeting of the Albany Congress was one of the earliest attempts to unite the colonies.

Philadelphia's Benjamin Franklin was one of the leaders of the Albany Congress. Franklin was a successful author, inventor, and statesman. He wanted the colonies to unite in a common government. A committee of **delegates** to the Albany Congress presented a "Plan for a General Cooperation of the North American Colonies." It called for the king of England to appoint a "president general" of the colonies. There would also be a "grand council" of representatives selected by the colonies. It would collect taxes and maintain an army. The plan turned out to be too ambitious for the colonies to approve. The Albany Congress ended without any plan for a union.

Franklin hoped his drawing would encourage colonists to see the importance of a union.

Braddock's Plan

The French controlled the Forks of the Ohio. The British government turned to General Edward Braddock to lead a force of British soldiers and colonial militia to seize Fort Duquesne. Braddock was an experienced

A FIRSTHAND LOOK AT
"JOIN, OR DIE"

On May 9, 1754, Benjamin Franklin published a drawing of a snake sliced into pieces. On each segment was the name of one of the British colonies. Underneath the snake were the words "Join, or Die." Franklin's meaning was clear. The colonies could never hope to survive if they didn't unite as one. The drawing has been called America's first political cartoon. See page 60 for a link to view it online.

General Braddock believed that British forces had nothing to fear from Native American attacks.

commander with more than 45 years of service in the army. But frontier fighting was new to him. Armies traveling in the unsettled parts of North America needed to move long distances through forests, over mountains, and across rivers. The lack of good roads made travel slow. Keeping armies supplied with food and equipment from hundreds of miles away was another challenge. Braddock's army would be facing an enemy used to such conditions. French Canadian militia and their Indian allies were experts at wilderness fighting. They were able to move swiftly and strike suddenly.

George Washington was now an officer on Braddock's staff. He had already learned these lessons. He tried to warn his new commander that war in North America would be different than war in Europe. But Braddock was unworried. The Native Americans, he said, "may, indeed, be a formidable enemy to your raw American militia, but upon the King's regular and disciplined troops, sir, it is impossible they should make any impression."

TODAY'S PERSPECTIVE

George Washington's actions in the French and Indian War gave him his first taste of fame. Newspaper reports helped make him a war hero throughout England's colonies. Today's historians are more aware of the mistakes he made as a young officer. Historian Joseph J. Ellis has written that Washington's battles with the French were "an education" in "the art of soldiering." The lessons he learned helped him become a better leader. "Instead of going to college, Washington went to war," writes Ellis.

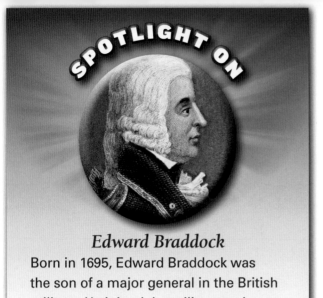

Edward Braddock

Born in 1695, Edward Braddock was the son of a major general in the British military. He joined the military at the age of 15 and served for more than 40 years before reaching the same rank his father once held. He battled against the French in the Netherlands in 1747. His vast experience led him to be sent to Virginia in 1755. He was tasked with commanding all of the British forces in North America.

The Battle of the Wilderness

In May 1755, Braddock and his army set off marching toward Fort Duquesne from Virginia on a 100-mile (161 km) journey across the Allegheny Mountains. They followed Washington's wagon road. But Braddock ordered his men to make the road wider as they went.

The Battle of the Wilderness was one of the first major conflicts of the French and Indian War.

Native Americans helped the French achieve victory in the Battle of the Wilderness.

He wanted to be sure that the road was wide enough to transport cannons from Virginia. They cut trees and moved boulders as they went. The going was so slow that some wondered if they would ever get to Fort Duquesne.

The French forces at the fort were growing stronger. There were already about 1,000 French troops defending the fort. They were being joined every day by more and more Indians from Canada and the Great Lakes region. Hundreds of warriors from the Ottawa, Ojibwa, Menominee, and Potawatomi Nations came to Fort Duquesne. Their tribes had been longtime trading

Braddock's wounds from the battle eventually resulted in his death.

partners and allies of the French. They had turned to the French in the past for protection from Iroquois raids. Now they were willing to fight alongside the French once again.

A force of 300 French Canadian troops and 600 Indians marched forward to ambush the advancing Braddock. They attacked Braddock's army as it marched through a heavily wooded area on July 9, 1755. The fight that followed became known as the Battle of the Wilderness. It was a complete victory for the French.

The British marched in columns four men across. This made them easy targets. The French and their Indian allies were able to take cover behind the trees and boulders that lined the trail. British soldiers fell to their gunfire. Braddock tried to rally his troops. But his forces had suffered too many **casualties**. He hoped to save his army by ordering a retreat. But he was badly wounded before he could leave the battlefield. Braddock died several days later while his army hurried back to Virginia. He was buried under the road he had helped build.

Braddock's men buried him on the way back to Virginia.

CHAPTER 3
PITT'S PLAN FOR VICTORY

The British took advantage of the opportunity created by the war to claim Acadia for themselves.

BRADDOCK'S MARCH WAS JUST

one of several British attempts to strike at the French in 1755. None of them were very successful. The French were able to stop most British advances in North America.

The exception came in a region of Canada called Acadia. Acadia was famed for its fertile soil. British colonists had long dreamed of expanding into the region. Acadia was already populated by French-speaking farmers and protected by a pair of French forts. The war gave New Englanders an excuse to push the farmers out of Acadia and claim the land for themselves.

British soldiers violently forced the Acadians out of their homes.

A force of Massachusetts militiamen and British soldiers attacked the French at Fort Beauséjour in June 1755. British cannon fire pounded the fort for days. The French were forced to surrender on June 16. Nearby Fort Gaspereau also surrendered to the British two days later. The British acted quickly after their victories to take complete control of Acadia. They confiscated property and farms. They also forced farmers out of their homelands. Entire families were loaded onto ships and relocated elsewhere in British-controlled areas of North America.

The French Strike Back

In 1756, France brought the conflict into British territory. The Marquis de Montcalm was a new French commander. He led an invasion of New York. He quickly captured two British positions, Fort Ontario and Fort Oswego. The forts were major losses for the British. Montcalm had used cannons captured from Braddock's army to capture the British forts.

The next target for the French was Fort William Henry at the southern end of Lake George in New York. The fort was important because it guarded a key water route into New York. In July 1757, Montcalm and his army arrived at the fort with heavy **artillery**. They surrounded the fort and offered the British a chance to surrender. The British refused. Montcalm began a relentless cannon barrage.

Fort William Henry was well constructed but small. It had been built to hold about 500 defenders. But there

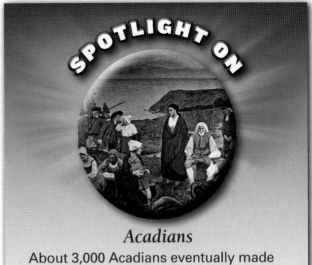

Acadians

About 3,000 Acadians eventually made their way to the bayous and marshes of southern Louisiana after being forced out of their homes in Canada. They established new communities there. Some tried to return to Canada. But they met with suffering or death at the hands of British forces.

The distinctive culture and dialect of the Acadians in Louisiana came to be called Cajun—a variation on the word *Acadian*. Today, the music and spicy food of the Cajuns are well known around the world.

Several Native American tribes aided the French at Fort William Henry.

were many more soldiers and civilians crowded inside. The overcrowding created unhealthy conditions. Soon everyone found themselves cut off from adequate water supplies. Disease spread rapidly inside the fort.

The British had used up almost all of their supplies and ammunition after two weeks of cannon fire. They raised a white flag of surrender on August 9. Montcalm told the fort's defenders that they would be allowed to leave as long as they surrendered their guns and promised not to fight against the French for at least 18 months.

But Montcalm had not cleared this plan with his native allies. They were unhappy with such generous terms of surrender. They believed that it was dishonorable for victors to return home from a battle without prisoners. Some of the natives attacked as the disarmed British prisoners left the fort. At least 69 of the prisoners were killed. More than 100 went missing.

Montcalm attempted to prevent the Native Americans from attacking the British prisoners, but was unsuccessful.

The Iroquois Confederacy

The nations of the Iroquois Confederacy formed the strongest alliance in North America before the Europeans arrived. Sometime around 1400, the leaders of five nations—the Mohawk, Onondaga, Cayuga, Seneca, and Oneida—agreed to follow a constitution called the Great Binding Law. They were joined by the Tuscarora Nation in 1722. The confederation became even stronger by trading with British and Dutch colonists for firearms. The Iroquois soon came to dominate most of the territory between Illinois and New York. Some 50,000 Iroquois live in the United States today.

Global Conflict

The conflict between Britain and France had grown into a global war. Both countries sought help from European allies. Soon much of Europe had entered the conflict. Austria, Spain, and Russia sided with France. The German states of Hanover and Prussia supported Great Britain.

The fighting was not limited to Europe. Both France and Britain maintained colonies on several continents. Some of those overseas colonies became battlegrounds in the war. By 1756, the conflict had spread to India, the islands of the West Indies, and elsewhere. This global war became known as the Seven Years' War. The fighting in North America was called the French and Indian War.

Things began going badly for Great Britain as the war's scope expanded. The British government turned

William Pitt saw the value of the colonial militias.

to new leadership in an attempt to reverse the course of the war. William Pitt became prime minister of Great Britain in 1757. Pitt recognized that Britain would need to send more troops into battle and spend more money if it hoped to win. He also wanted to rely more heavily on American colonists to defeat the French in North America. Most British military leaders looked down on the colonial militias as undisciplined and undependable. But Pitt urged his commanders to treat the militias well and keep them well supplied.

The first test of Pitt's plan came at Louisbourg, a French fortress on Cape Breton Island in Canada. This impressive stone fort stood watch over the mouth of the St. Lawrence River, the main water route into Canada. Some called it the "key to Canada." Louisbourg was defended by about 6,000 French troops and 400 cannons. Pitt attacked with more than 15,000 British and colonial troops.

British warships circled Louisbourg. This cut the fort off from supplies and reinforcements. Then British cannons began firing away at the walls of the fortress. The fort was nearly in ruins six weeks later. Many of

British ships prevented the French at Louisbourg from escaping or receiving reinforcements.

its buildings were in flames. The French defenders surrendered. The British prepared to drive deeper into the heart of Canada.

Another massive British force was gathering hundreds of miles to the west to take the French Fort Carillon on Lake Champlain. The British had an enormous advantage in numbers. They brought an army of 12,000 to attack the fort. The Fort was defended by only 3,000

British soldiers stormed Louisbourg from the shore.

French and Indians. But French commander Montcalm deployed his troops wisely. He formed defensive lines behind a barrier of sharpened logs called an abatis. The British suffered terrible casualties when they tried to storm the French lines. One soldier said his comrades "fell like pigeons" to the French and Indian fire. The British finally gave up and retreated after repeated attempts to break through. They had suffered a loss of

Fort Carillon was built by the French between 1755 and 1759. It was later renamed Fort Ticonderoga. The fort played an important role in both the French and Indian War and the Revolutionary War. Much of it has been preserved as a historic landmark. See page 60 for a link to find out more about the fort's history and learn how you can see it for yourself.

2,000 dead or wounded men. The French had lost fewer than 400 men.

Despite that setback, Pitt's plan was beginning to pay off for the British. The size of the British forces in North America was beginning to wear down the French. A force of British colonials won a bold and important victory at Fort Frontenac on Lake Ontario in August 1758. Capturing the fort brought the British a treasure of badly

The British scored a major victory at Fort Frontenac.

The British took over Fort Duquesne as the French fled.

needed supplies and weapons, including 76 cannons. It also put a large British force in a key strategic position between Canada and the French forts in the Ohio River valley. Now the British could block any attempts by the French to send supplies and reinforcements from Canada to their forts.

The French soon realized that they needed to withdraw from the Ohio River valley. They retreated from Fort Duquesne at the Forks of the Ohio in the fall of 1758. They destroyed the fort as they left. It had been more than four years since George Washington's defeat. The British at last seized the Forks. They rebuilt the fort and named it after William Pitt.

CHAPTER 4
THE FALL OF QUEBEC

The British went up against strong defenses at Quebec.

THE BRITISH VICTORIES AT

Fort Frontenac and Fort Duquesne opened the way for an invasion of Canada. A British fleet began to sail up the St. Lawrence River in the summer of 1759. It was bound for the French Canadian capital of Quebec. The fleet was commanded by James Wolfe. It was made up of some 200 ships and 9,000 soldiers. It hoped to defeat the French army, capture Quebec, and end the war.

The French were not worried. They believed that the city's defenses were strong enough to resist the British. Quebec stands atop a rocky **bluff**. The bluff's point pokes out into the St. Lawrence River like a wedge. The town's defenders could take cover behind a wall nearly 20 feet (6 meters) high and several feet thick.

Quebec's name comes from an Algonquian word meaning "the river narrows here." The St. Lawrence becomes narrow at Quebec. Its currents also become dangerously unpredictable. This posed a challenge to enemy ships trying to navigate the river. The British had tried to capture Quebec in previous wars with France. But they had failed three times. The city's natural defenses and the river's tricky currents had always frustrated the British. Montcalm believed that this attack would be no different.

At first, it appeared that Montcalm was right. The huge British **armada** arrived in Quebec in June. Wolfe

Quebec's location, high on a bluff, made it difficult to attack.

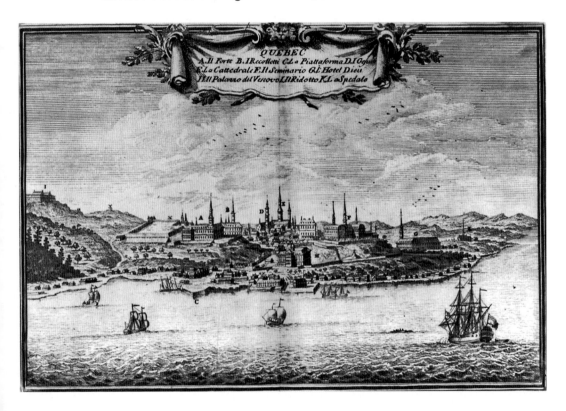

James Wolfe carefully planned his attack against Quebec.

set up his camp across the river from the city. He made several attacks on the city over the next several weeks. Each attack was fought off by the French. The French were content to remain safely behind the city's thick walls. All the British could do was continue pounding away at Quebec's fortifications with cannon fire. The defenders endured the battering and held strong.

By September, Wolfe knew that he didn't have long to find a gap in the French defense. The harsh Canadian winter would arrive soon. This would spell doom for any invasion force.

Wolfe and his men used a hidden path to sneak into Quebec.

Then Wolfe got the break he so badly needed. He discovered a lightly defended path leading from the riverbank up the steep bluff to the walls of Quebec. Wolfe ordered a nighttime crossing of the river to surprise the few French soldiers guarding the path.

The surprise attack worked. British troops scrambled up the path to the top of the bluff under the cover of darkness. Montcalm awoke on September 13 to find 4,000 British soldiers in neat ranks outside the gates of Quebec. He made a quick decision. The French would make the first move instead of waiting for the British to attack. Montcalm marched his soldiers out from behind the safety of the city's walls to a flat stretch of land called the Plains of Abraham. The two armies faced each other across the open countryside. A loud cheer went up from the French as they began marching straight toward the long line of red-coated British soldiers.

British officers ordered their troops to hold their fire as the French approached. There would be no wasted gunfire. They would wait until the enemy was close enough for the soldiers to take careful aim. Finally, the British fired when the French had come within 40 yards (37 m) of their lines. Dead and wounded French soldiers fell to the ground. Their attack came to a halt and quickly turned into a rapid retreat. The British charged

The French retreated in the face of heavy British fire.

Wolfe's men mourned his death.

after the fleeing French soldiers with their bayonets ready. Both Montcalm and Wolfe suffered fatal wounds in the combat. The British swept the French from the battlefield so quickly that a French officer later wrote: "No rout was ever more complete than that of our army."

The British marched into Quebec on September 18 and raised their flag over the city. The pivotal battle of the French and Indian War had ended. So had France's dreams of an empire in North America.

The war went on for several more years. But France was practically defeated. The British scored major victories at Detroit and Montreal in 1760. Britain also won victories over France in the West Indies, Germany, and India.

France and Britain were ready for peace by 1763. Both nations were weary after the long war they had waged around the world. They were also broke. The cost of fighting the wars so far from home had emptied their national treasuries. In 1763, they signed a treaty called the Peace of Paris. It made Great Britain the clear winner. The treaty gave Britain control of Canada and all French lands east of the Mississippi River. It also gave Britain control of Florida, which had previously belonged to Spain.

Europe's powers divided up North America. But they failed to consider the Native Americans who already lived there. The war's end did little to benefit the native

A VIEW FROM ABR⭐AD

It took weeks for news to travel on ships from North America to Europe. People in England did not learn of the British victory at Quebec right away. All of England celebrated the news by ringing church bells, firing cannon salutes, and lighting bonfires. They also mourned James Wolfe's death in the battle for Quebec. In a speech to Parliament, William Pitt compared Wolfe to the greatest heroes of ancient history. One newspaper stated, "[T]rue courage never appeared more glorious than in the death of the British Wolfe."

A FIRSTHAND LOOK AT
THE PEACE OF PARIS

The 1763 Treaty of Paris was also known as the Peace of Paris. It brought about an official end to the French and Indian War and secured Great Britain's control over North America. Representatives from Great Britain, France, Spain, and Portugal signed the document. See page 60 for a link to read the document online.

nations. The French forces were gone from North America. English settlers poured over the Appalachian Mountains in search of land. They violated treaties that had promised to respect Indian homelands.

Colonists began settling along the Ohio River after the end of the French and Indian War.

Some Indians struck back. Pontiac was a leader of the Ottawa people. He led a war against British settlements around the Great Lakes. Warriors from the Ojibwa, Potawatomi, Wyandot, and other nations joined his fight. Soon the frontier was a scene of frequent clashes between settlers and natives.

In 1763, King George III of England announced the Proclamation Act. This act prohibited colonists from settling west of the Appalachian Mountains. It was intended to prevent conflict between settlers and Indians. But the waves of settlers moving west could not be stopped for long. Fighting between Indians and white settlers in North America continued for more than a century.

SPOTLIGHT ON

Pontiac

Born around 1720, Pontiac was a leader of the Ottawa people. He dreamed of a united effort by many Native American nations to defend their homelands against Europeans. He followed the teaching of a Delaware prophet named Neolin. Neolin encouraged Native Americans to avoid European goods and customs. Pontiac led attacks on the British in 1763. These attacks came to be known as Pontiac's Rebellion. But Pontiac was unable to force the British out of the Great Lakes region. He was murdered in 1769.

What Happened Where?

Ohio River Valley Both France and Great Britain hoped to control the Forks of the Ohio, the present-day site of Pittsburgh, Pennsylvania.

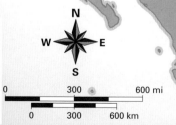

| British |
| French |
| Spanish |
| French/British disputed land claim |
| Spanish/British disputed land claim |

N
W ✧ E
S

0   300   600 mi

0   300   600 km

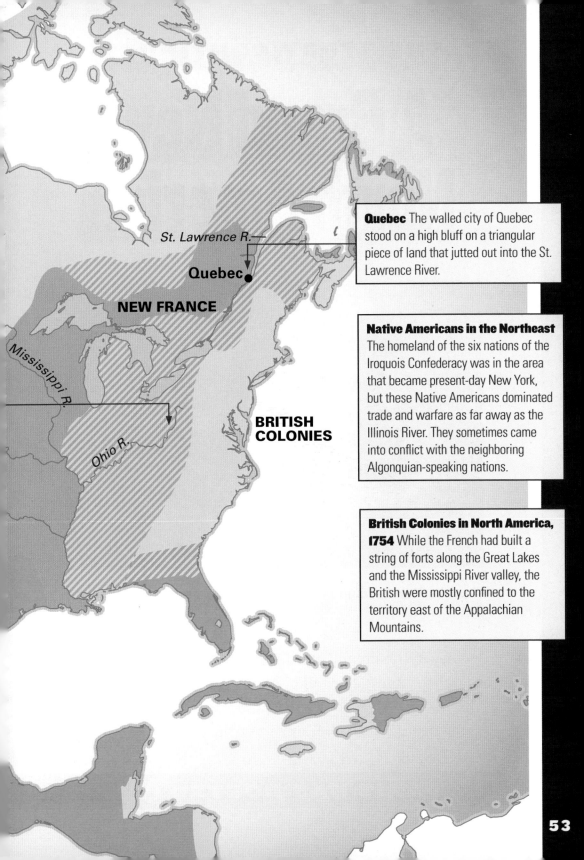

St. Lawrence R.

Quebec

NEW FRANCE

Mississippi R.

Ohio R.

BRITISH COLONIES

Quebec The walled city of Quebec stood on a high bluff on a triangular piece of land that jutted out into the St. Lawrence River.

Native Americans in the Northeast The homeland of the six nations of the Iroquois Confederacy was in the area that became present-day New York, but these Native Americans dominated trade and warfare as far away as the Illinois River. They sometimes came into conflict with the neighboring Algonquian-speaking nations.

British Colonies in North America, 1754 While the French had built a string of forts along the Great Lakes and the Mississippi River valley, the British were mostly confined to the territory east of the Appalachian Mountains.

A Brand New North America

The American Revolution pitted the colonists against the British military.

Victory in the French and Indian War gave the British complete control over all of North America east of the Mississippi River. The French and Spanish settlers living in Canada and Florida became minorities under British rule.

The costs of fighting the war in so many places so far from home had drained the British treasury. Defending the new territory from Native Americans would be a costly expense. The British government began placing taxes on everything from tea to sugar to newspapers in order to pay these expenses.

Many of the colonists were outraged by the taxes. They complained that it was unfair for the British government to tax the colonies when they were not represented in the British Parliament. The colonists' dissatisfaction with Great Britain grew. The American Revolution began just over 10 years after the war ended.

The French and Indian War also resulted in major changes to the relationship between Native Americans and Europeans. With the French gone from America, many native peoples began to set aside their differences and see themselves as part of a larger group. This was a major step for many of them. To these people, other native groups were just as foreign as the French were to the British or the Spanish. Native peoples began to think of themselves for the first time not just as members of different tribes and nations, but as part of one group: Native Americans.

Robert Dinwiddie

Edward Braddock

King George II (1683–1760) was the king of Great Britain during the Seven Years' War.

Robert Dinwiddie (1693–1770) was the lieutenant governor of Virginia at the time of the French and Indian War.

Edward Braddock (1695–1755) was a general who led the British at the Battle of the Wilderness. He died from wounds suffered in the battle.

William Pitt (1708–1778) was the prime minister of Great Britain who helped lead his nation to victory in the war.

Louis-Joseph, Marquis de Montcalm (1712–1759) was the French general who won victories at Fort Oswego and Fort William Henry. He was defeated in the battle for Quebec and died of wounds suffered in the battle.

Pontiac (ca. 1720–1769) was the Ottawa leader who led a Native American war against the British in 1763.

James Wolfe (1727–1759) was the British general who led his troops to victory at Quebec, but died of wounds suffered in the battle.

George Washington (1732–1799) was the colonial officer whose actions caused the earliest conflict in the war. He later led the American Revolution and served as the first president of the United States.

George Washington

TIMELINE

Pre-1400	1607	1608	1722

Pre-1400
Seneca, Cayuga, Onondaga, Oneida, and Mohawk Nations form the Iroquois Confederacy.

1607
Jamestown, Virginia, is the first British colony in North America.

1608
Quebec is founded.

1722
Tuscarora join Iroquois Confederacy.

1756	1757	1758	1759

1756
French take Fort Oswego and Fort Ontario; Great Britain and France formally declare war.

1757
French capture Fort William Henry; William Pitt becomes prime minister of Great Britain.

1758
British capture Fort Duquesne and rename it Fort Pitt.

1759
British capture Quebec.

1750

King George II grants land in Ohio country to businessmen who form the Ohio Company.

1754

May 28
Washington leads a successful surprise attack on the French.

Albany Congress meets in June and July; Washington surrenders at Fort Necessity on July 4.

1755

June 16
Fort Beauséjour surrenders to the British.

July 9
Braddock is defeated in the Battle of the Wilderness.

1760

Montreal surrenders to the British.

1763

Peace of Paris is signed; King George III issues a proclamation setting boundaries for the new territory in North America.

LIVING HISTORY

Primary sources provide firsthand evidence about a topic. Witnesses to a historical event create primary sources. They include autobiographies, newspaper reports of the time, oral histories, photographs, and memoirs. A secondary source analyzes primary sources, and is one step or more removed from the event. Secondary sources include textbooks, encyclopedias, and commentaries.

Fort Ticonderoga Formerly known as the French Fort Carillon, Fort Ticonderoga played a role in both the French and Indian War and the Revolutionary War. It has been preserved as a historic landmark. For information on how to see the fort, visit *www.fort-ticonderoga.org /index.htm*

"Join, or Die" Benjamin Franklin's 1754 drawing of a snake sliced into pieces is often called America's first political cartoon. You can view the cartoon by visiting *www.loc.gov/pictures/resource /cph.3g05315/*

Peace of Paris The Peace of Paris, also called the Treaty of Paris, ended the French and Indian War and secured Great Britain's control over North America. You can read the text of the treaty by visiting *http://avalon.law.yale.edu/18th_century/paris763.asp*

The Redeemed Captive Returning to Zion Rev. John Williams wrote a book about his experience as a French captive many years before war was declared. You can read excerpts from his book at *www.americancenturies.mass.edu/collection/itempage. jsp?itemid=7777*

Books

Day, Nancy. *Your Travel Guide to Colonial America*. Minneapolis: Runestone Press, 2001.

Englar, Mary. *The Iroquois: The Six Nation Confederacy*. Mankato, MN: Capstone, 2000.

Gard, Carolyn. *The French and Indian War: A Primary Source History of the Fight for Territory in North America*. New York: Rosen, 2004.

Gray, Edward G. *Colonial America: A History in Documents*. Oxford: Oxford University Press, 2003.

Horn, Bernd. *Battle Cries in the Wilderness*. Toronto: Dundurn, 2011.

McClung, Robert M. *Young George Washington and the French and Indian War, 1753-1758*. North Haven, CT: Linnet Books, 2002.

Smolinski, Diane. *Battles of the French and Indian War*. Chicago: Heinemann Library, 2003.

Smolinski, Diane. *Soldiers of the French and Indian War*. Chicago: Heinemann Library, 2003.

Web Sites

Canadian Museum of Civilization—Virtual Museum of New France
www.warmuseum.ca/cmc/explore/virtual-museum-of-new-france
Read about French adventures in colonial Canada.

Historical Society of Pennsylvania—French and Indian War Primary Sources
www.hsp.org/default.aspx?id=639
View a collection of journals and maps related to the war.

PBS—The War That Made America
www.pbs.org/thewarthatmadeamerica
Learn more about the French and Indian War at this companion site to a PBS series.

GLOSSARY

alliances (uh-LYE-uhns-iz) agreements to work together for some result

armada (ahr-MAH-duh) a large fleet of warships

artillery (ar-TIL-uh-ree) large, powerful guns that are mounted on wheels or tracks

bluff (BLUHF) a high, steep cliff

casualties (KAZH-oo-uhl-teez) people killed or wounded during warfare

colonies (KAH-luh-neez) areas settled by people from another country and controlled by that country

delegates (DEL-i-gitz) representatives to a convention or congress

militia (muh-LISH-uh) a group of people who are trained to fight but who aren't professional soldiers

missionaries (MISH-uh-ner-eez) people who travel to spread their religious faith among others

neutral (NOO-truhl) not taking either side in a war

stockade (stah-KADE) a defensive wall made of posts set in the ground

INDEX

Page numbers in *italics* indicate illustrations.

ABOUT THE AUTHOR

Andrew Santella is a journalist and author. His work has appeared in publications such as the *New York Times*, *GQ*, and *Slate*. He is the author of many books for young readers.